Original title:
Under the Christmas Tree's Star

Copyright © 2024 Creative Arts Management OÜ
All rights reserved.

Author: Penelope Hawthorne
ISBN HARDBACK: 978-9916-94-384-7
ISBN PAPERBACK: 978-9916-94-385-4

A Festive Tale of Love

In a cozy nook, the lights flicker bright,
An elf in a costume wobbles in sight.
Cookies for Santa, now crumbs all around,
While dogs steal the turkey that's just been browned.

The ornaments dance as the cat takes a leap,
With a flick of her tail, the tinsel goes sweep.
Grandma in slippers, she laughs with delight,
As the kids plan a snowball fight in their sight.

A reindeer disguise makes a cousin feel bold,
He prances and twirls, in a shirt that is gold.
Mom rolls her eyes, with a grin on her face,
"Next year, let's skip all this silly embrace!"

Yet laughter fills air, like the snowflakes that fall,
With each silly moment, we hold on to all.
Though chaos may reign, love's the gift that we keep,
In this festive tale, we find joy, not just sleep.

The Language of Winter's Embrace

Snowflakes whisper secrets neat,
Gossiping where children greet.
Hot cocoa spills, we all laugh bold,
As snowmen shiver, their noses cold.

Polar bears wear silly hats,
While penguins dance like chubby cats.
Sledding fails, we tumble down,
In this frosty, funny town.

A Wonderland Beneath the Branches

Gumdrop forests beckon sweet,
While gingerbread men tap their feet.
Elves play tricks with candy canes,
And reindeer prance during silly games.

Tinsel tangles bring us glee,
As we try to climb a tree.
Laughter echoes in the night,
While cats chase lights, what a sight!

Tales of Warmth and Cheer

Grandma's knitting flies through the air,
As yarn becomes a fuzzy bear.
Cats climb high, their tails a mess,
While all of us just laugh, no stress.

Popcorn flies upon a dare,
Wreaths that mold without a care.
Socks go missing, oh where's that pair?
In this chaos, love's always there.

Reflections in the Firelight

Crackers pop with festive glee,
And silly hats dance on our knees.
The cat gets caught in the holiday lights,
While everyone giggles at innocent sights.

Marshmallows roast, a sticky fight,
As the fire crackles bright tonight.
One bounces back with fluffy cheer,
Making memories that we hold dear.

Where Time Stands Still

Beneath the lights that twinkle bright,
Grandpa snores loud on this Christmas night.
The cookies we baked now disappear,
While the cat's caught a mouse, oh dear, oh dear!

The tree leans left, a bit too bold,
It sways with tales it never told.
A tangled mess of ribbons and glee,
Who tripped on the tinsel? Was it me?

The Gentle Touch of Kindness

A gift wrapped tight with tape galore,
Uncle Bob swears he saw a snore.
We laugh and dance in cookie crumbs,
While Aunt May shouts, 'Shh! Here he comes!'

The dog steals a bite from the feast,
And the kids yell, 'He's not a beast!'
With kindness here, and laughter too,
This holiday cheer feels fresh and new.

A Snow-Dusted Reverie

The snowflakes swirl like a wild dance,
'Til Timmy slips, still in his pants.
The sled rolls by, a glorious trip,
As Dad joins in with a silly flip!

Mom's cocoa spills, a marshmallow fight,
While penguin pajamas bring such delight.
Laughter echoes through frosty air,
Our winter wonder, a carefree affair.

Navigating the Path of Joy

With socks mismatched, oh what a sight,
We gather 'round, hearts feeling light.
The board games stretch long into night,
But who will claim that final bite?

We argue if reindeer can really fly,
While Aunt Sue plays Santa, oh my, oh my!
In this mayhem, love's simple, it's clear,
Together we giggle, year after year.

Secrets Wrapped in Velvet Dreams

A shadow lurks by the slumbering pine,
Whispers of wishes mixed with fine wine.
Tinsel tangled in the cat's eager paw,
Twinkling lights give a snooze to the floor.

Presents piled high, a real sight to see,
A hamster escapes, Oh what a decree!
Bows flying off like holiday gifts,
While grandma giggles, who needs any rifts?

Radiance of Frosted Memories

Sugar cookies dance on the table so wide,
While Uncle Fred dons his festive glide.
Eggnog spills like a jubilant cheer,
As the dog steals a present, oh dear!

Wrapping paper rockets aimed at the moon,
Giggling children hum a jazzy tune.
Wrapping the cat just for fun,
Who knew Christmas could add to the run?

Beneath the Celestial Ornament

Thoughts of silent night now float in the air,
As Dad wears the star, sings without a care.
The tree stands tall with a wonky lean,
While siblings squabble, who's the best seen?

Magic wrapped in a bow that won't stay,
Jokes that fly like reindeer on display.
Grandpa's snore blends into the tune,
As we hope he wakes up soon!

Lullabies of Evergreen Serenity

Frothy cocoa spills on the carpet below,
While the cat climbs high to join the show.
Socks as gifts, oh what a surprise,
With jingle bells ringing 'til morning's rise!

A partridge in a box, quite an odd pick,
As laughter erupts with every silly trick.
The sound of joy fills the merry home,
Signaling another wild Christmas tome!

The Echo of Silent Nights

In the middle of the night,
A sock fell down, quite a sight.
The cat gave a jump, lost her cool,
Chasing shadows, like a fool.

Laughter echoed through the halls,
As we dodged invisible balls.
Grandma's snoring meets the fun,
Silent nights? Yeah, right, we're done!

Gifts of Laughter and Love

Wrapped in paper with no care,
A gift that squeaks, we pause and stare.
Uncle Joe opened it wide,
A rubber chicken slipped inside!

Banter flies from hand to hand,
These quirky gifts, oh, they are grand.
With giggles shared, we find delight,
Loves and laughs on this cold night.

Celestial Dreams in the Dark

Star-shaped cookies, a baking spree,
Frosting smiles for all to see.
A joke or two with every bite,
Sugar rush, what a wild night!

Elves in slippers dance around,
While Dad attempts to make a sound.
He sings off-key, we all just cheer,
His grand finale? A half-baked deer!

When Pine Scent Meets Magic

Pine needles scatter, what a mess,
Decorating is quite the test.
A tinsel trap, a sparkly sneak,
Dad gets tangled—oh, what a freak!

The lights blink fast, a disco show,
Uncle spins, tries to steal the glow.
We laugh, we cheer, a goofy crew,
This holiday spirit, how it grew!

The Glow of Winter Dreams

In winter's chill, we dream and scheme,
With socks and snacks, we plot our theme.
A sneaky elf with a cheeky grin,
Hiding the cookies, oh where's the win?

The mistletoe hangs, a hazard zone,
Uncle Fred trips, now we moan and groan.
The lights blink out in wild delight,
As Grandma's cat takes flight tonight.

Secrets Wrapped in Ribbons

Presents piled high, but what's inside?
A pair of socks? Oh, what a ride!
The kids shake boxes to hear the sound,
Daring each other with joy unbound.

A sweater knitted, with love and care,
But it's two sizes too big to wear.
We laugh and giggle at all the fuss,
As Auntie's fruitcake earns a big 'no thanks' plus.

Where Frosted Wishes Dwell

In snowball fights, we find delight,
While snowmen sway, their eyes too bright.
Carrots disappear, where could they be?
The dog just grins, all covered in glee.

Hot cocoa spills, the marshmallows float,
As we debate the best cookie tote.
Jingle bells ring and laughter soars,
As Dad dons reindeer horns, oh what a chore!

Lights of Joy and Memory

The twinkling lights flash green and red,
While Dad trips over the tree instead.
We stand back giggling, a true holiday sight,
As Mom yells, 'Don't touch! That's not quite right!'

The stockings hang, like puppets in flight,
Each one stuffed; it's a glorious sight.
But who stole my candy? I see it there,
A mouse with a grin and a piece of pear!

Glimmering Echoes of Yuletide

When lights twinkle bright and cats do pounce,
Amidst all the toys, they do announce.
A treasure of laughter, the children squeal,
As ornaments tumble and chaos we feel.

With cookies half-eaten, we giggle and sigh,
As Santa's big belly struggles to fly.
The reindeer all laugh, they munch on the treats,
While grandpa gets stuck in the tightest of seats.

A Tapestry of Hope and Cheer

Garlands of giggles, and silly sweet hats,
Grandma's old stories, mixed up with the cats.
We dance like the elves in mismatched old shoes,
And sing off-key tunes that nobody could refuse.

The snowman outside sports a crazy wide grin,
With buttons for eyes and a mouth made of tin.
As we toss snowballs, the laughter does fly,
Who knew wintery fun could be such a high?

The Gift of Silent Snowflakes

Snowflakes are falling like glitter from clouds,
While kids build a snowman, all wobbly and proud.
They haul in the carrots, and rocks for the eyes,
But soon it starts melting—what a big surprise!

Hot cocoa spills over as we take a big sip,
On marshmallow boats we set sail on a trip.
The dog makes a splash, and the cocoa does fly,
Now we're each wearing—can't guess why?—a pie!

Reflections in the Holiday Hearth

Old stockings are hung, but they all look askew,
Each filled with strange treasures, not a single shoe.
There's socks filled with gadgets, and candy that shines,
While Dad cracks a joke about last year's designs.

In the glow of the fire, we gather around,
With tales of old mischief, and laughter profound.
Through all of the whispers, the warmth of our cheer,
Is wrapped snugly close as we ring in the year.

Underneath the Glittering Canopy

Beneath the lights so bright and merry,
A cat climbs up, gets stuck, oh dearie!
The cookies vanish, crumbs in their wake,
Santa's sleigh? Just a makeshift cake!

The gifts are wrapped with lots of flair,
But the dog thinks it's his new spare chair!
Tinsel's tangled with a funny twist,
Even the ornaments jump with a twist!

The Spirit of Giving

The sweater Aunt June made, too bright, too bold,
Yet we wear it proudly, like treasures untold.
The fruitcake returns, again on the shelf,
Sneaky re-gifting? We're all in on it ourselves!

We write our cards with shiny gold pens,
And try not to spill while making new friends.
Each gift we want, seems to come with a laugh,
Like socks for the dog, or a potato as half!

Enchanted Nights and Twinkling Eyes

The lights flicker like a disco ball,
The kids make snow angels at the mall.
As laughter echoes, they slip and slide,
Even Granny's trying to take a ride!

With hot cocoa spills and marshmallow fights,
We dance around in our silly tights.
Cookies catch fire? It's all part of the game,
When the holiday cheer ignites our name!

A Symphony of Yuletide Joy

The carols start off tune, but we sing loud,
With jingle bells ringing, we're quite the crowd.
The tree leans over, it's seen better days,
Yet we celebrate in our amusing ways!

Gift wrap battles end with paper on the floor,
As we unwrap treasures we never asked for!
Laughter and giggles fill up the air,
In this crazy season, we float like a pair!

A Canvas of Dreams and Joy

Twinkling lights on the branches sway,
As cats plot mischief, come out to play.
Presents stacked high, a precarious sight,
Will they topple? Oh, what a delight!

Grandma's fruitcake, heavy like a rock,
One bite might just cause a loud clock!
The kids all giggle, eyes wide with glee,
Wishing for snacks, and maybe a tree!

Advent of Whispers and Wishes

Neighbors gossip about gifts galore,
As kids sneak peeks, they can't take it anymore.
Santa's sleigh might need a new map,
After last year's 'oops,' we heard the mishap!

Grandpa's snoring like a bear in the den,
Sweet dreams of cookies, he'll dream again.
A nose so red, it shines like a light,
Can anyone tell him it's just Frosty tonight?

Where Magic Meets Memory

Ornaments jingle like merry little bells,
Each tells a story of laughter and spells.
A dancing elf knocked over a chair,
Oops! It's okay, it adds to the flair!

The cookies are gone! Who could be so bold?
Evidence shows; it's a sight to behold!
The dog's left paw prints all over the floor,
At least he didn't bring in anymore!

The Laughter of Holiday Spirits

Tinsel flying like it's in a race,
Kids rolling on the floor, what a wild place!
Wrapping paper turns to a battlefield,
Who will emerge with a treasure revealed?

A festive scarf draped around the cat,
Is she a gift now? Or just a doormat?
Laughter echoes, as the story unfolds,
In this jolly chaos, happiness holds!

Crystal Reflections of Holiday Hopes

Presents piled high, oh what a sight,
A cat in a box, what a silly fright!
Tinsel tangled up like a jolly old maze,
We laugh till we drop in holiday craze.

Cookies left out, oh dear, what a smell,
Santa's on a diet? We can't really tell!
Rudolph's red nose, a beacon of cheer,
But where is my gift? Did it just disappear?

The Essence of Laughter and Light.

Elves with big shoes dance all around,
Leaving sparkles and giggles, no frown can be found.
Snowflakes like feathers float down from the sky,
While I slip on the ice, oh my, oh my!

Hot cocoa spills over, marshmallows afloat,
With a splash and a dash, we all start to gloat.
Chasing each other like kids in the snow,
Is it laughter or mischief? It's hard to know!

Beneath Twinkling Lights

The lights are all dancing, such a sight to behold,
Even the squirrels have stories to be told.
The star on the top has a shy little grin,
While I'm busy fighting a tangled string spin.

Strange holiday sweaters make everyone laugh,
Uncles are arguing on holiday math!
One cookie for you, then two for me here,
Who ate the last slice? Oh dear, oh dear!

Whispers of Holiday Magic

Gifts wrapped in paper, like colorful bugs,
Tugging on ribbons, we all get the shrugs.
The turkey is singing, or is that a dream?
We giggle and snicker, or so it would seem.

Boots left by the fire are no longer neat,
As socks start to vanish, oh what a feat!
Whispers of joy fill the chill in the air,
With laughter and cookies beyond any compare.

Illuminated Dreams of December

Twinkling lights dance on walls,
A cat leaps, plotting its falls.
Wrapping paper strewn on the floor,
As grandma snags her foot on the door.

Cookies left without a trace,
While Uncle Joe sported a funny face.
A flurry of socks, not a pair to find,
It's chaos here, but oh so kind!

Pine needles itch on my nose,
With every wink, more laughter grows.
A cheeky elf with a jelly belly,
Dances the jig, just so silly!

Tangled lights, but who won't care?
With giggles that fill the frosty air.
Each glance shared a holiday cheer,
In December's glow, we gather near!

Enchantment Beneath Glittering Skies

Laughter spills like cocoa warm,
While puppy runs with festive charm.
Grandpa snoozes with a snore,
Dreaming of snacks he can't ignore.

Wreaths hung crooked, what a sight,
As little cousin takes a bite.
Mistletoe hanging above their heads,
Uncle Fred trips, oh, what he dreads!

Tinsel tangled in my hair,
I just can't seem to get a spare.
A popper crackles with a loud bang,
As Aunt Lily bursts into a sang!

Snowmen wobble, hats askew,
With goofy noses, it's quite the view.
The magic of cheer, funny and bold,
With stories of joy, never getting old!

Melodies of an Everlasting Night

Songs of laughter drift through halls,
While Fido fetches wrapped up balls.
A clumsy dance with jingle bells,
As grandkids share their playful yells.

An ornament drops, oh a cheer!
While Mom tries hiding her beer.
The fireplace crackles, what a sight,
With marshmallows flying in delight!

The carolers knock, but what a tune,
Singing off-key, under the moon.
A grandma busts out the eggnog, too,
With tipsy hugs from all of you!

Yet through the giggles and crazy spins,
In silly moments, true joy begins.
Together we bask in this shining light,
Sharing our love through this funny night!

The Warmth of Kindred Spirits

Gathered round, we share our cheer,
With aunties and uncles all drawing near.
Cousin's toy train goes off the tracks,
As laughter erupts with goofy quacks.

Card games played, oh what a mess,
As drinks spill forth, who could guess?
With jokes exchanged like warm wishes,
And memories caught in our favorite dishes.

A paper crown sits askew on my head,
With whispers and giggles, we all spread.
A toast to the wild, sweet memories made,
With every sip, a joy cascade.

With mischief glinting in our eyes,
We cherish the moments that never dies.
In the warmth of friends, hearts beat in tune,
Under bright lights, we'll sway till June!

The Lullaby of Snowflakes

Snowflakes dance like tiny elves,
Spinning round with silly yelps,
Frosty giggles in the air,
Wishing for a snowball flare.

Cocoa mugs and marshmallow hats,
A plop of joy from frosty mats,
Tumbling, rolling, a snowy spree,
Who knew flakes could be so free?

Chasing tails in swirling bliss,
Find a flake, you can't miss,
A snowman grinning, nose of coal,
Winks and cracks, that's his roll!

So come and join this snowy fun,
Laughter echoes, one by one,
In the chill, we find a treat,
Snowflakes dance with jolly feet.

Embrace of Frosty Tales

Frosty breezes whisper low,
Socks on hands, oh what a show!
Giggling shadows, snowball fights,
Chasing joy through frosty nights.

A Reindeer lost his jingle bell,
Thought it hid beneath the shell,
Found it in his buddy's stew,
Oh, what a silly thing to chew!

Carrots flying, a hat with flair,
Frosty dances without a care,
Tiptoe through this frozen tale,
Where laughter's light will never pale.

Whispers shared in snowflake light,
Silly friends beneath the night,
Let's build dreams in winter's sea,
With frosty hugs and jubilee!

Dreams Wrapped in Warmth

Blankets piled with cozy cheer,
Whispers soft for all to hear,
Pillow fights and giggly screams,
Wrapped in warmth of happy dreams.

Candles flicker, shadows play,
Tickle fights that last all day,
Marshmallows dance on fires so bright,
In jolly jest, we own the night.

Sneaky snacks from hiding spots,
Munching loudly, oh what plots!
Chasing crumbs, oh what a sight,
Silly faces, pure delight.

With cocoa sips and laughter spilled,
Chasing joys, our hearts are filled,
In these moments, all we need,
Dreams wrapped up, our souls freed!

Mystical Nights of Giving

Elves appear with cheeky grins,
Wrapping presents made from bins,
Puppies barking, oh what fun,
Sneaky paws on the run!

Twinkling lights in ludicrous ways,
Cat's in the tree, oh what a craze,
Shattering baubles on the floor,
Restless nights, forevermore!

Stockings hung with crafty flair,
Hidden treats beside the chair,
Toys that giggle, wiggle, and squeak,
Making our holiday quite unique!

Together we share this joyful dance,
In winter's laugh, we take a chance,
In the glow of playful jest,
These mystical nights, we are blessed!

Dreams Nestled in Tinsel

Joyful dreams dance and prance,
Wrapped in shiny paper's chance.
Elves with cookies, oh so sweet,
Gifts that tickle little feet.

Snowflakes tumble from above,
While reindeer play in icy glove.
Stockings hung with toys galore,
Who needs sleep? There's so much more!

Laughter spills like cider's warmth,
As kittens find their cozy charm.
Beneath the glimmering delight,
We giggle till the morning light.

So grab your hat, let's dash around,
With candy canes to hunt and found.
In this wonderland so bright,
We weave our silly holiday night.

Mirth Beneath the Glistening Boughs

The tree is twinkling with great cheer,
But Grandpa snores; oh dear, oh dear!
He thought he'd sneak that extra pie,
But now he dreams of flying high.

Cats are perched on every limb,
Trying their luck, a festive whim.
A dog in reindeer antlers prances,
While biscuits fly in joyful dances.

Glitter spills from playful hands,
As kids create their snowy plans.
The lights are blinking in a race,
Who can spot the silliest face?

With giggles bouncing off the walls,
We capture joy in holiday calls.
Each ornament tells a funny tale,
Of all the ways we might derail.

The Essence of Holiday Wonder

Sparkling bulbs, a sight to see,
Uncle Joe climbs the ladder with glee.
He's looking for a way to latch,
To hang those lights that never match.

Cookies left for Santa's cheer,
A glass of milk—unless that's beer?
Sister's snorts as she sneaks a treat,
Her giggles send the kittens in heat.

Ornaments rescued from the past,
Each a memory that won't hold fast.
A fish in mittens, can you believe?
That's holiday spirit, we can't deceive!

As we layout our festive spread,
We cheer as Auntie pops her head.
"Where's the turkey?" she shouts in glee,
But we just laugh—there's ham, you see!

Chronicles of Frost and Firelight

Stories told beside the flame,
Of mischievous elves who play a game.
Pine needles fall as laughter swells,
Each tale spun with magical spells.

Hot cocoa spills from tiny hands,
As grandparents recount their plans.
Little ones giggle, eyes so wide,
While Aunt Sue divides the rum and pride.

Snowmen made with scarves and hats,
Playing tricks on outdoor cats.
With noses bright and buttons round,
Their giggles echo all around.

So here's to cheer, in every room,
While blessings blossom, heart and bloom.
We'll toast our cups to the joy we find,
In every laugh, forever entwined.

Threads of Joy in Evening's Embrace

Tinsel tangled in my hair,
I dance around, unaware.
My cat leaps high, thinks he can fly,
In the chaos, I just sigh.

Cookies baked but burnt to brown,
Santa's stuck, can't lose his crown.
A present pops, it's not my fault,
It's a trick, or just a jolt!

Lights that flicker, strange and bright,
Freak me out in the quiet night.
I step outside, mouth open wide,
The neighbors see and laugh with pride.

With cocoa spilled on brand new socks,
We trade our tales and silly flocks.
In laughter shared, we find the cheer,
As mischief dances, we persevere.

Frost-Kissed Moments of Magic

Snowflakes drift, a silent tease,
I slip and land, oh what a freeze!
My scarf wraps tight, a cozy mess,
I thought I'd win, but guess who's less?

Eggnog flows like slippery glue,
A sneaky sip, and now I'm blue.
The dog runs off with a gift in tow,
Chasing him leads to a snowy show!

Lights that twinkle like a disco ball,
I dance around, but trip and fall.
The tree leans left, I think it's fate,
A holiday hug, oh no, too late!

With laughter loud, we toast with glee,
And curse the cat perched by the tree.
In frosty fun, we find a way,
To merry up this wacky day.

Lanterns of Love in the Chill

Candles wobble, wax drips low,
While I sing out, oh what a show!
Grandma claps, but can't keep time,
Next year's dance shall be sublime!

Ornaments hang, each telling tales,
Of family mishaps and holiday fails.
A rogue string of lights just popped,
And off I go, as laughter hopped.

Snowman smiles with a strange hat,
A carrot nose drawn by the cat.
With mittens mismatched, we spin around,
In this cozy craziness, chill is found.

As lanterns glow and warmth is near,
We toast to joy and festive cheer.
With hearts aglow, we're all a part,
Of funny moments, joy at heart.

A Symphony of Red and Green

Gingerbread men all gone awry,
Didn't think they'd fly so high!
I chase them down, that sneaky crew,
Why'd I bake a dozen, who knew?

Ribbons tangled, fights of cheer,
The wrapping paper, oh dear, oh dear!
A present falls, it bounces back,
Looks like my gift-wrapping skill's out of whack!

The dog finds joy in shiny toys,
While kids collide with squeals and noise.
We deck the halls and lose our minds,
In this funny tangle, laughter binds.

A symphony of red, all mixed with green,
We dance around in this festive scene.
With joyful hearts, we sing with glee,
In every mishap, we find jubilee.

Glimmers of Hope in the Dark

When the lights blink and fade away,
Cats dance around like they're on display.
Tinsel tangled in the family pet,
Laughing at chaos, we have no regret.

Snowflakes fall, creating a scene,
The neighbor's lawn looks far too obscene.
With laughter echoing through the night,
Merry chaos brings pure delight.

Uncle Joe's jokes make us cringe in pain,
As Aunt Sue's soup brings laughs like rain.
Each silly moment grins and sways,
Filling our hearts in unexpected ways.

So gather 'round and cheer with glee,
For moments like these, we all agree.
In the dark, our spirits cling tight,
Glimmers of hope shine ever so bright.

The Richness of Family Bond

With wrapping paper all over the floor,
Grandma sneaks in to snag some more.
We giggle at secrets, we trade our gifts,
In this chaos, our love truly lifts.

Cousins are plotting a grand prank tonight,
Dads making bets on who'll win the fight.
Who can resist pie with a side of fun?
In our little world, we're forever one.

Siblings share bites of their latest snacks,
Why is the dog on the table? Relax!
Each chuckle and whisper, each glance, each grin,
With every mishap, our kinship grows thin.

So gather together, let's cherish this cheer,
In the laughter and chaos, nothing to fear.
With each silly moment that we create,
The richness of family—it's never too late!

A Radiance of Memory and Warmth

A snowman with lopsided eyes stands proud,
His carrot nose hidden beneath a shroud.
Kids skip about, their laughter a song,
In this nightly magic, we all belong.

Mismatched socks and hats all askew,
The joy in our hearts makes winter feel new.
Memories sparkle, each silly affair,
Sharing our stories, the laughter we share.

As cookies disappear, we can't find the stash,
Mom feigns annoyance while making a splash.
Dad's silly dance moves get all of us rolling,
In this game of love, our hearts keep on strolling.

So let's drink cocoa with marshmallows galore,
Laugh 'til we drop; can we ask for more?
In the glow of our memories, we find our way,
A radiance of warmth, forever we'll stay.

The Comfort of Shared Moments

With hot cocoa mugs in our chilly hands,
We huddle together, forming new plans.
Gifts wrapped with bows, yet not quite the same,
We giggle at blunders that bring us more fame.

Aunt Beth's old sweater—too many bright hues,
Either you love it or just hide your views.
A dance-off erupts, the rules thrown away,
With each silly shimmy, we keep dismay at bay.

Stories shared late 'til the moon bids adieu,
With laughter and smiles, we share our truth.
Each moment a treasure, each grin a jewel,
Together we conquer, together we rule.

So let's embrace this fun, wild spree,
In these bundled up moments, we're truly free.
For comfort in laughter, we keep on our quest,
The comfort of sharing—oh, we are blessed!

The Color of Joyful Anticipation

Little socks hung with care,
Hoping for gifts that are rare.
Giant bows sprout like weeds,
While cats plot their mischievous deeds.

Chasing ribbons that dance and twirl,
Around the room the chaos will swirl.
Cookies crumble, frosting on faces,
Santa's list lost in our races.

Tiny hands reach for the delight,
As wrapping paper takes off in flight.
Inevitably, someone spills juice,
While untouched gifts are at their truce.

Joyful giggles fill the air,
As we pretend not to care.
The sweet scent of pine and cheer,
Marks the season we hold near.

Echoes of Laughter Beneath the Boughs

Tinsel fights with furry paws,
As we laugh at all the flaws.
Paper crinkles, excitement grows,
While Dad trips over tangled bows.

Nibbling cookies, crumbs in our hair,
We sneak peeks while pretending to care.
A sneeze, a cough, and gifts go fly,
As we search the room like spies on high.

Hiding toys in a clever spot,
Grandpa argues with the hot pot.
With every laugh, the night takes flight,
Under starlight, everything feels right.

Amid the chaos, joy will bloom,
In this quiet holiday room.
Echoes of laughter fill the space,
Creating memories we can't replace.

Rays of Light in Winter's Embrace

Flashes of lights blink in glee,
As snowmen dance in jubilee.
With mismatched socks and silly hats,
We invite all the bouncing cats.

The tree sparkles bright and bold,
With stories of secrets yet untold.
Grandma's dance brings giggles galore,
While we pretend to snore and snore.

Ornaments swing, a clumsy ballet,
As grandkids launch into their play.
In every corner, a surprise awaits,
Like fruits on the table—who will make plates?

As we sip cocoa, warm and sweet,
We savor every laugh and treat.
In this space draped in marshmallow white,
We find joy in our shared delight.

Glistening Joy and Silent Nights

Glistening dreams wrapped up tight,
Whispers of joy in the night.
Silly hats fly when we're not looking,
While gingerbread men end up cooking.

Snowflakes dance, each unique and funny,
As we unwrap gifts worth a ton of money.
Laughter bubbles like hot cocoa foam,
In this wild, whimsical home.

Cats knock down the brightest lights,
Creating more festive delights.
Every mishap is a tale to tell,
As we trip and laugh through the night's spell.

In this cozy nook, spirits soar,
Where happiness walks through every door.
Glistening moments glint in the night,
As we bundle our dreams, warm and tight.

Starry Nights and Quiet Moments

Twinkling lights in every corner,
A cat's tail swishes, oh what a humdinger!
Beneath the glow, we sip warm cheer,
Spilling cocoa, as laughter draws near.

Eager kids in bright pajamas,
Debating who's on Santa's dramas.
The sugar cookies disappear fast,
Little stowaways, we hope they won't last!

A present unwrapped, oh what's inside?
It's just a sweater, but we all still smiled.
Wrapped up in crinkles, chaos and cheer,
Finding joy in gifts, both far and near.

With every giggle and playful tease,
We dance through the night, as we please.
Starry moments in the laughter's embrace,
Creating memories no time can erase.

Echoes of Joy in the Chill

Frozen noses and chilly toes,
Making snowmen with tiny clothes.
Kids dash out, making a scene,
Snowballs fly; it's a wintery dream.

Inside we smell the pine and spice,
Giggling at cousins—oh, isn't that nice?
Grandma's stories make us all snort,
As we try to guess just what we'll report.

A mishap with lights gets a good cheer,
As Dad falls back, with holiday beer.
We laugh out loud, it's too much to take,
A Christmas tale for the memory's sake.

With echoes of joy filling the room,
We gather 'round, dispelling gloom.
In each heart, a memory's sound,
In the merry moments, love is found.

Beneath a Canopy of Hope

Up above, lights shimmer and sway,
A dance of laughter leads the way.
Old ornaments tell tales of the past,
While new ones crash; oh what a blast!

Pet puppy unwraps the best gift yet,
Chasing ribbons, without a regret.
He's the star; he steals the show,
While we sip cider, feeling the glow.

Our gingerbread house, oh what a sight,
Melting away in a sugary fight.
Sweet chaos reigns, and who needs plans?
When fun calls out, we take our stands.

Around the glow, we share our dreams,
With giggles and giggles, laughter beams.
In messy moments, our hearts take flight,
Beneath the magic of this wondrous night.

Journey of the Evergreen Heart

Headed out to find the perfect fir,
While Dad claims he's the best, oh dear!
With saw in hand, and an adventurous cheer,
We hunt for a tree that won't disappear.

Back home we bicker on how it should stand,
Twisted and crooked, a sight so grand.
Decorations hang in every wrong place,
Yet it holds a charm we all must embrace.

Tinsel flies as we let out a squeal,
Unwrapping gifts with zeal, what a deal!
Mom's wrapping paper is a sight to see,
Like a tornado has danced through the tree.

But through all the chaos and light-hearted fun,
Deep in the heart, the joy has begun.
In this journey of laughter, love is the aim,
Wrapped in laughter, we play the same game.

Illumination of Forgotten Dreams

In the corner, lights twinkle bright,
A cat's got the ribbon, what a sight!
Old dreams jump out, dancing with glee,
While Dad tries to climb that old, wobbly tree.

Forgotten toys, they come alive,
Santa's list? We'll surely revise!
Uncle Joe's gift? A bright, squeaky toy,
It's a laughing stock, not meant for joy!

A fruitcake sits, as stale as can be,
Yet Grandma swears it's the best recipe!
A tug-of-war with holographic ties,
As everyone bursts into sugar-coated cries.

In this chaos, we spot the delight,
A mishmash of cheer, all perfectly right!
With giggles and snacks, we deck the halls,
Who knew laughter could echo through walls?

A Festival of Light and Love

Tinsel and laughter, oh what a sight,
Grandpa dancing, showing his might!
Cats jump high with ornaments clinking,
While kids try to stay awake, but are blinking.

Cookies are hidden, under the plate,
Elf on the shelf? I think he's late!
Everyone's guessing what's in that box,
I hope it's not those weird, old socks!

Lights tangled up, a true Christmas feat,
As we trip over each other's feet.
A relay for wrapping, it's chaos divine,
With laughter so loud, our hearts intertwine.

We raise our mugs, with cocoa so sweet,
In this riot of fun, we've found our beat.
A festival of joy, with stories galore,
More love in the air than we could ever store!

The Journey of Wishes and Warmth

A sleigh rides past, or maybe it's Ted,
Wearing a hat that's far too red!
Wishes fly, on paper wings,
As we ponder the joy that this holiday brings.

The nightly game of 'guess that gift',
Uncle Bob's ideas give everyone a lift.
Pine-scented mischief fills up the space,
'Tis the season to laugh, not a usual face!

A reindeer's joy, bright, tickly and grand,
Is really just a laugh from the neighbor's band.
A journey of dreams, as wild as it seems,
Creates a magic dipped in sweet whipped creams.

With frosty cheers and giggles galore,
We find warmth in laughter, who could ask for more?
As wishes are granted with giggly delight,
We'll chase them in shadows, till the last light.

Frost-Kissed Tidings

Frosty flakes tumble, a ballet divine,
While Aunt Tina's socks somehow collide!
An elf's on a mission, dancing in fate,
With a bowl full of treats, that's never too late.

The tree wobbles, like Grandma's old truck,
We laugh as it leans, what's the odds of bad luck?
Mirth in each corner, amidst the bold cheer,
Let's not forget that soft drink from last year!

In mismatched sweaters, we twirl in delight,
As Grandma's mischief keeps us up all night.
A turkey groans as the clock strikes eight,
We dive for the pies—it's an epic debate!

With frost-kissed air and hearts all aglow,
We dance and we sing, in this wondrous show.
Each moment a treasure, each giggle a feast,
In this festival madness, we find solace at least!

Haikus of Hearth and Heart

In jolly spirit,
Elves trip over their own feet,
Gifts wrapped like cats play.
Tinsel in my hair,
Sparkles dance while we all sing,
Jokes fly through the air.

Mistletoe's a trap,
Kisses mean a sticky face,
Laughter fills the room.
Cookies burn, oh no!
Smoke alarms join in the fun,
Fire drills on the go!

Kids sneak peeks, oh dear,
Hiding presents is so tough,
Wrapping paper wars.
Socks match with great flair,
But only when I step out,
Left with one of each.

Cheers and giggles roar,
Family finds the best puns,
Love wrapped up so tight.
In the glow of lights,
Dance around like silly fools,
Heartfelt joy ignites.

Delicate Wishes in the Twilight

Frosty windows glow,
Candies stuck to every face,
Sugar rush at dawn.
Socks hung with great care,
But somehow fall every year,
Santa's sneaky tricks.

Warm mugs of cocoa,
Slurps and spills on favorite,
Sweaters full of cheer.
Family dance-off time,
Who can twirl without a crash?
Giggles fill the air.

Sprinkled snow outside,
Sledding down the block so fast,
Winter's giggly ride.
Snowmen lose their heads,
Thanks to playful puppy paws,
Who knew fluff would roll?

Whispers in the night,
Wishes tossed like shooting stars,
Dreams of candy canes.
Laughter echoes loud,
Happy hearts all round the clock,
Even grumpy cats.

Candles Flicker with Warmth and Wonder

Lighting up the room,
Candles dance as shadows play,
Flames drawn in a swirl.
Fuzzy socks and hugs,
Hot chocolate spills do abound,
Froth upon our lips.

Jingle bells in tune,
Cats chase the sparkly bows,
Tinsel trails behind.
Gifts that make no sense,
A toaster? Why yes, of course,
Every year, the same.

Trees wear garland crowns,
As dogs chew on the branches,
Canine cuteness reigns.
Laughter and delight,
From tales of Christmases past,
Grin through every bite.

Dad's dressed as Saint Nick,
Twirling funny little jokes,
Though his beard won't stick.
Echoing bright cheer,
Delighted hearts take a bow,
Fun's the only rule.

A Dance of Joyful Memories

Stomping through the snow,
Making angels as we fall,
Snowflakes on our tongue.
Sneaky little kids,
Peeking at an open gift,
Presents wrapped with love.

Cousins playing pranks,
Faking falls on the slick floor,
Fake slips turn to laughs.
Whirls of joy abound,
Holiday cheer dances light,
Jokes that feel so right.

Wonky Christmas hats,
Three sizes too big, of course,
Worn with goofy pride.
Pictures with big grins,
Silly faces, blooper reels,
These moments make us.

Clinking mugs we share,
Toasting all that we've been through,
Joy wrapped 'til next year.
Together we will sing,
Melodies of playful hearts,
Love, our final prize.

Hope Illuminates the Night

Hope glows bright like Rudolph's nose,
It leads us where the laughter flows.
Beneath the branches, we find delight,
As we tumble around in festive light.

Jingle bells echo, socks on the floor,
Grandpa's dance moves leave us wanting more.
A feast of cookies, a mountain high,
Santa's on a break, oh my, oh my!

Pine needles tickle as we spread cheer,
The cat steals tinsel, never sincere.
With puns and giggles, we sing off-key,
Joy wrapped in laughter, oh can't you see?

So let's toast marshmallows, watch snowflakes twirl,
As silly sweaters around us swirl.
Those moments of joy, let nothing interfere,
When hope shines bright, we have no fear!

Eternal Light of Togetherness

Chasing shadows with the brightest smiles,
We gather 'round, adding to our piles.
With uncle's jokes and grandma's cheer,
The warmth of togetherness fills the sphere.

Wreaths on doors, and lights so loud,
Dad's got his antlers, feeling so proud.
We laugh at mishaps, spill cocoa too,
What a sight, in our festive zoo!

Gifts wrapped tight, some go in reverse,
Oh no, not grandma's new bag of verse!
But laughter overflows, filling the space,
A comedy show, no need for grace!

So grab your hat and join the fray,
With jokes and stories, we'll dance the day.
In this festive chaos, a light shines bright,
Unified in laughter, our hearts take flight!

A Garden of Holiday Dreams

In a garden where giggles blossom and bloom,
We plant seeds of laughter, making room.
With elves on the shelves doing headstands,
And candy canes traded for random bands.

Snowflakes tumble like sugar dropped low,
While kids chase each other in grand snow throw.
A snowman with shades and a funky hat,
Declares himself king, while we all just chat.

Cookies sprout like flowers here and there,
It's a race to eat, with crumbs everywhere.
Laughter and giggles take center stage,
In this garden of dreams, we turn the page.

So sip on your punch and strike up a tune,
Let's make merry 'neath the big silver moon.
With smiles and fun, we can't go wrong,
Just fertile ground for our silly song!

The Rhythm of December Hearts

Jingle bells echo, creating a beat,
A waltz of cookies, a rhythmic treat.
With hearts prancing, all wrapped in bows,
We dance with joy as the fireplace glows.

Hats askew while we flail and spin,
Holiday spirits ready to win.
Mismatched socks, the style today,
In our December parade, we just sway!

Mistletoe mishaps, it's a comedy scene,
With uncle slipping, and cousin's routine.
The clock strikes twelve, we cheer all night,
It's the rhythm of laughter; it feels so right.

So raise your glass, toast the zany bunch,
As we savor every cookie and munch.
For in this dance of hearts, we find,
The goofy memories, forever entwined!

Starlit Paths of Anticipation

With twinkling lights that dance and play,
The cat has found the wreath today!
Zooming past the gifts with glee,
Who knew that bows were meant for me?

Cookies vanish in a flash,
While we hide gifts with a crash!
A sneaky elf with lots of flair,
Has wrapped our secrets everywhere!

Whispers float of what's to come,
As laughter echoes, oh so fun!
A cousin trips, and down he goes,
We laugh harder than he knows!

With mischief and cheer, the night won't end,
As we chase each other, and hearts will mend!
This magic moment, we hold it dear,
For every giggle, let's toast right here!

Echoes of Laughter in the Night

In a sea of red and vibrant green,
The funniest sights are yet to be seen!
A grandpa's joke, a quirky rhyme,
Has us rolling over laughing every time!

Grandma's hat, so big and bright,
Wobbles as she takes a bite!
The dog is wearing mistletoe,
We all lean down, but where to go?

With silly hats and jingle bells,
We trade our stories, who's got tales?
A hot cocoa spill, oh what a show,
Laughter bubbles, it's time to glow!

When midnight strikes, the fun expands,
A conga line begins, just as planned!
Twirls and spins, we dance with flair,
Uniquely funny, no one could compare!

The Glow of Togetherness

In cozy corners, warmth does spread,
With socks that clash, and slippers red!
We gather close for tales and cheer,
As giggles rise, they disappear!

Wrapped up tight in snuggly bliss,
Who knew that socks could lead to this?
A duel unfolds with goofy grace,
As pillows soar, it's quite the race!

With games galore and chocolate treats,
We stomp and clap our dancing feet!
The joy of being, side by side,
With friendly banter, we take pride!

Under blankets, giggles abound,
In every heart, the love's profound!
With lights a-glimmer, joy unfolds,
Togetherness, a treasure manifold!

Unwrapping Treasures of Time

With paper flying, chaos reigns,
The dog thinks gifts are all for gains!
Teddy bears and socks galore,
What will we find behind this door?

An awkward dance, a present slips,
And laughter erupts from joyful quips!
A sweater that's two sizes too wide,
We laugh until the tears collide!

Hidden gems and wobbly toys,
The shrieks of laughter from the boys!
Each layer peeled, the joke unfolds,
A rubber chicken, as the story told!

With memories made, we hold them dear,
In our hearts, they'll always be near!
Unwrapping laughter, joy, and glee,
Time's the best gift, shared with thee!

The Heartbeat of December

Jingle bells and candy canes,
A squirrel stole my chocolate gains.
I chased him round the living room,
Now he's dancing to my favorite tune.

Snowflakes fall, I slip and slide,
I hope the neighbors don't decide.
To peek outside and see my fall,
I'm the laughingstock, after all.

Eggnog spills, I toast my hat,
The family cat thinks it's a mat.
He lounges on my favorite chair,
This festive chaos fills the air.

With gifts piled high, I hear a crash,
Not my fault, just a playful dash!
The dog runs off with my best sock,
December fun, oh what a flock!

Shadows of Evergreen

In the corner, a tree stands tall,
But ornaments? I dropped them, all!
A careful balance, doomed to fail,
I watch as they pick the perfect bail.

Gifts wrapped tight, a puppy chews,
Holy night, I have no shoes!
Santa's list, I find a mix,
He's got my name scribbled in ticks.

The lights blink like they know my fate,
I chuckle as I set the plate.
But cookies vanished in a snap,
I blame the elf with a wobbly cap!

With laughter loud, the carols play,
Last year's mishaps come back to stay.
Each joyful moment bottled tight,
A memory made, in cheerful delight.

A Tapestry of Cheery Moments

Mittens stuck, I can't find one,
Lost in laughter, oh what fun!
The lights, they twinkle, makes me grin,
As I wrap yarn and let chaos win.

Presents stacked like a wobbly tower,
Uncle Bob is snoring, what a power!
He'll wake up just in time for pie,
With whipped cream on his cheek, oh my!

Kids are racing, a gift does roll,
It crushes Dad's last potato chip bowl.
Thunderous laughter fills the room,
Dancing shadows chase the gloom.

Crazy hats and socks askew,
The spirit's wild, just like our crew.
With every smile, joy is shared,
In the warmth of love, we are ensnared.

Wishes in the Winter Air

Wishes fly on winter's breath,
Uncle Joe's jokes, we stand in death.
A misfit gift of sprouting socks,
He wraps them up in glittered boxes.

Nibbled treats leave crumbs in trails,
The cat now wears the elf's old veils.
Around the corner, giggles erupt,
As Aunt Lucy tries to step, then trips.

Cinnamon scents waft through each room,
While dad attempts to use the broom.
Sweeping up a sparkly mess,
He chuckles at his clumsiness.

With roaring laughter, we'll toast tonight,
These festive moments filled with light.
A wild holiday, full of cheer,
Our joyful chaos brings us near.

Whispers of the Winter Night

In a corner, a gnome comes to play,
Sneaking cookies, much to our dismay.
He trips on the lights, does a funny jig,
While the cat just stares at this goofy pig.

Frosty nibbles on candy canes,
As Santa's sleigh takes all the reins.
Rudolph snorts, looking a bit perplexed,
He can't find his nose—maybe it's next!

In the hush of snowflakes falling down,
A squirrel dons a tiny red crown.
He shimmies and shakes, all decked in flair,
Turning friendly with a hat-wearing bear.

With giggles echoing all through the night,
We're wrapped in laughter, oh, what a sight!
Men in reindeer suits take a pie,
As the mischievous elf gives a wink and a sigh.

Sparkle of Midnight Wishes

The elf swings high, hanging from a tree,
Spilling decorations as he yells, "Whee!"
With glitter in his beard and tinsel on toes,
We wonder if he really knows where it goes.

A snowman with shades, feeling quite cool,
Complains about winter, breaks every rule.
At midnight he dances, it's quite a show,
While children are dreaming, his moves steal the glow.

Socks filled with goodies, they wobble and sway,
A parade of toys that just want to play.
Bouncing and rolling, they tumble with cheer,
Bringing us laughter and holiday cheer!

With cookies and cocoa, we gather in glee,
As the partridge discusses the best Christmas tree.
On this whimsical night, so merry and bright,
The fun never ends, not until morning light.

Beneath the Twinkling Lights

Twinkling bulbs start to spin round,
While a polar bear wears a tutu, unbound.
He dances with joy, clumsily tripped,
As the ornaments shimmer, on tree limbs they zipped.

A raccoon in PJs raided the stash,
Eating all cookies with a loud, crunching smash.
While kids giggle softly, a prank in the air,
A stocking now sings—oh, what a flair!

Chimneys are covered in glitter and fluff,
As jolly old St. Nick claims, "I've had enough!"
He leaps on his sleigh, ready for flight,
But slips on snowflakes and giggles in fright.

With cocoa in hand, we gather so tight,
To share in the fun beneath colorful light.
A night filled with laughter, and joy we can't see,
As the magic unfolds—come join, won't you be?

Shadows Dance in Holiday Glow

The shadows are dancing, oh what a scene,
With elves doing limbo, so silly and keen.
Santa's lost track of the cookies he packed,
As a penguin balances, a bit out of whack.

Reindeer play cards, with snacks piled high,
A game of 'Go Fish' under dark winter sky.
They laugh 'til they snort, it's quite the delight,
As the moon peeks through, casting glow in the night.

With tinsel on their tails, they prance and they twirl,
While frosty friends giggle, and give it a swirl.
The tree shakes its branches, with laughter so sweet,
As the shadows embrace this joyous retreat.

So gather your spirits on this bright, funny eve,
With dances and giggles that we won't believe.
In this holiday wonder, all hearts lift and soar,
As we sing out with glee, forever wanting more!

Milton Keynes UK
Ingram Content Group UK Ltd.
UKHW021950151124
451186UK00007B/171

9 789916 943847